Mel Bay Presents

MW00387119

Easy Celtic Solos for Fingerstyle Guitar

by Lisle Crowley

CD CONTENTS

1	Banks of the Suir [2:09]	8	The Liverpool Hornpipe [:33]
2	The Bantry Girls Lament [1:42]	9	Merrily Kiss the Quaker [1:06]
3	The Boulavouge [1:50]	10	O Danny Boy [3:34]
4	Dingle Regatta [:55]	11	Red is the Rose [2:19]
5	The Doon [2:15]	12	Star of the County Down [2:37]
6	Father Kelly's Jig [1:53]	13	Wellington's Advance [1:23]
7	Lanigans Ball [1:32]		

1 2 3 4 5 6 7 8 9 0

Visit us on the Web at www.melbay.com — E-mail us at email@melbay.com

ABOUT THE AUTHOR

Lisle Crowley lives in Southern Utah and is the Head of the Guitar Department at Dixie State College of Utah. He also teaches private guitar lessons at Roland Lee's Guitar Gallery. He has been arranging guitar books since 1995, penning over 10 books and recording accompanying CD's. Lisle's original compositions and arrangements have been featured in *Fingerstyle Guitar* magazine as well as the Guitar Gallery CD sampler. Lisle has also released a solo CD *On A Clear Day* and the critically acclaimed *High Desert Duo* CD with Cellist Robin Keith. Lisle is becoming known around the nation for his thoughtful arrangements, sensitive playing, and his wonderful compositions.

You can visit Lisle on the web at: www.lislecrowley.8m.com.

AUTHORS NOTES

Many of these songs are arranged in two or three sections. The first section is the easiest to play and is marked with an **A**. The second section is marked with a **B** and is more advanced. If there is a third section it will be marked with a **C** and will be the most advanced section of the arrangement. The beginning student should be able to play section **A** and have a very nice fingerstyle solo. The advanced student should be able to play all sections. By arranging the pieces this way I have found that I am able to satisfy all my students and challenge them at the same time. I've arranged some of my favorite Irish numbers in this book and I hope you enjoy them as much as I do.

THE BANKS OF THE SUIR

THE BANTRY GIRL'S LAMENT

BOULAVUGUE

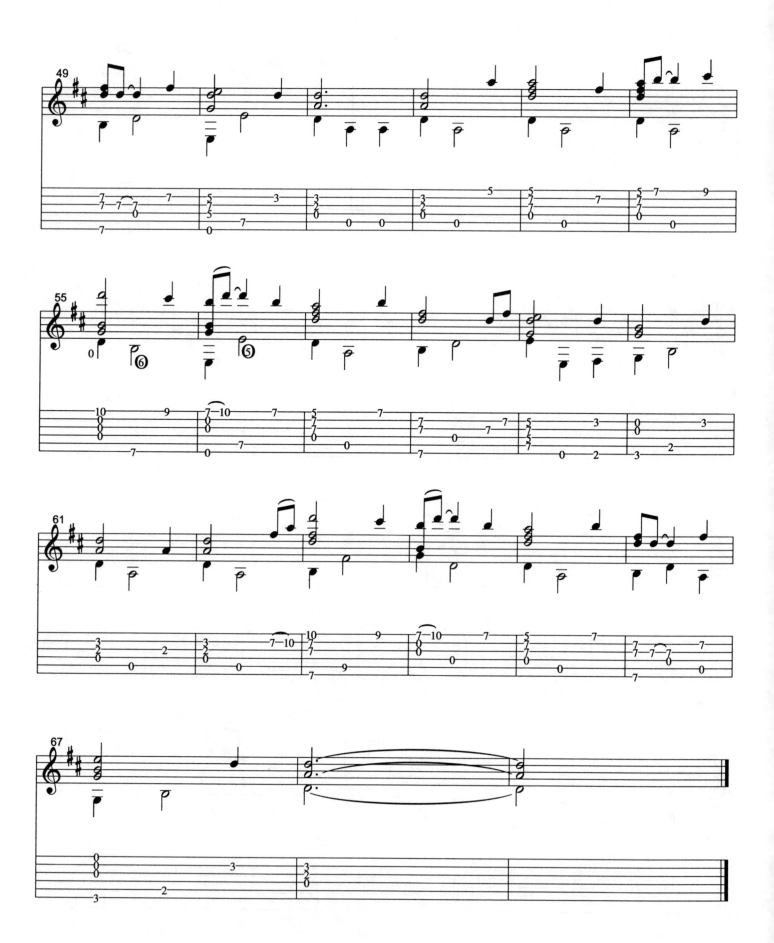

10

DINGLE REGATTA

13

THE DOON

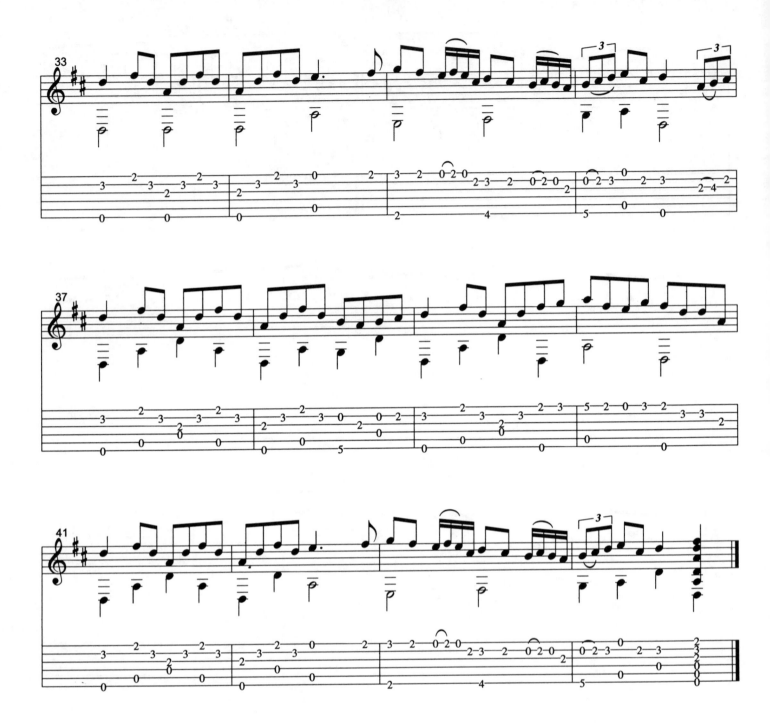

FATHER KELLY'S JIG

LANIGAN'S BALL

THE LIVERPOOL HORNPIPE

MERRILY KISS THE QUAKER

O DANNY BOY

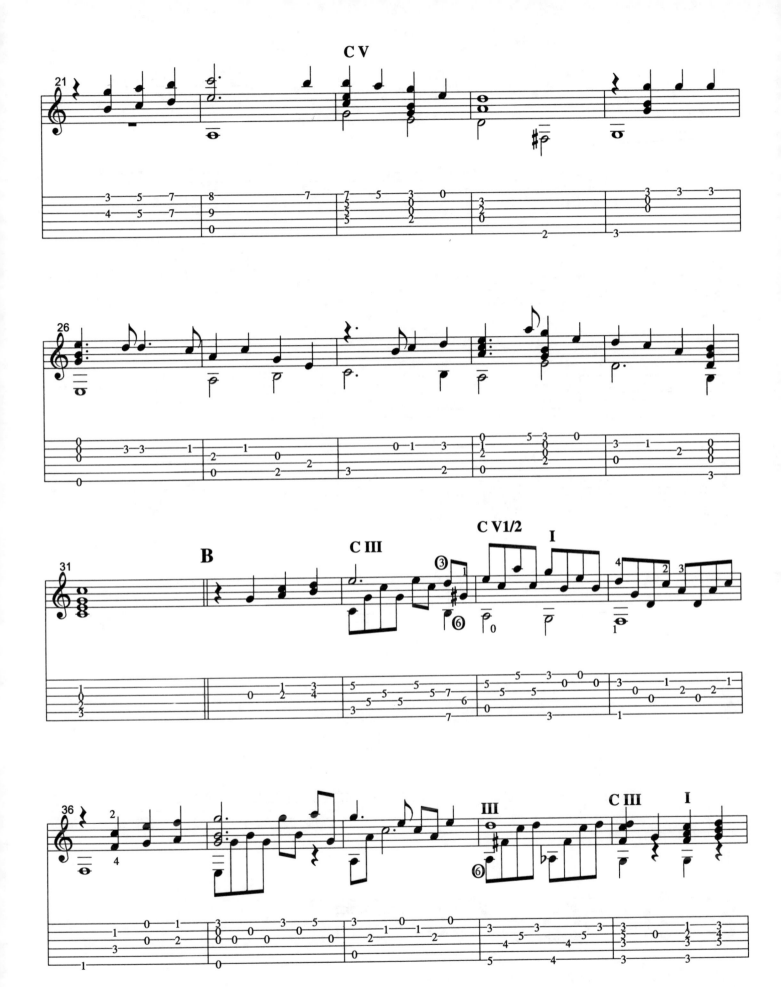

29

RED IS THE ROSE

⑥=D

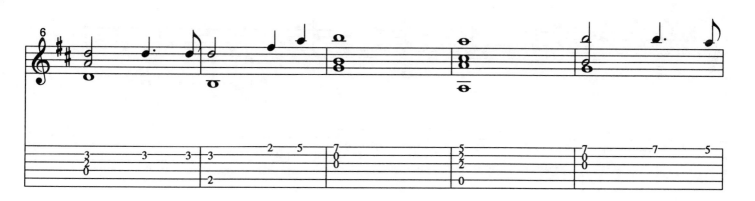

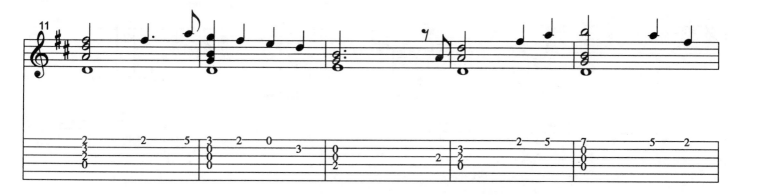

32

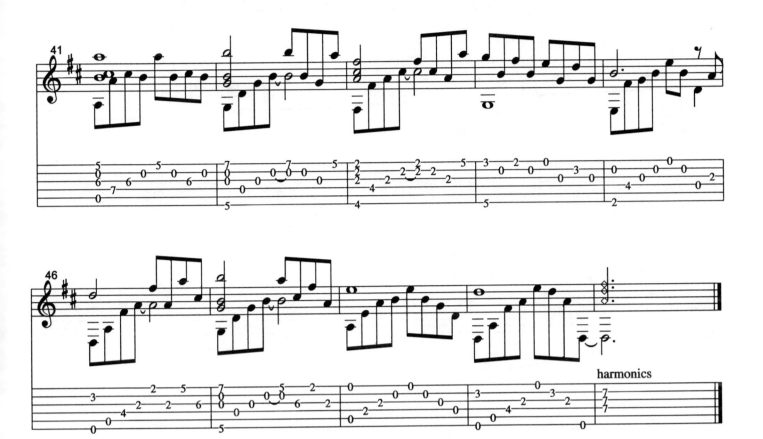

STAR OF THE COUNTY DOWN

WELLINGTON'S ADVANCE

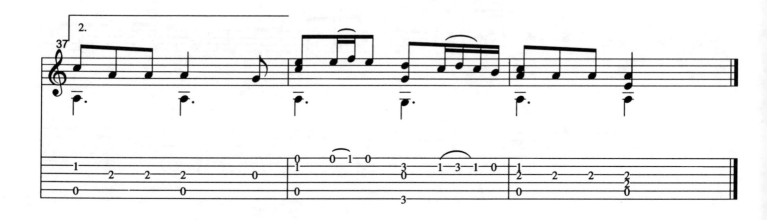